The Story of Alexander Fleming

Alan Trussell-Cullen

www.Rigby.com
1-800-531-5015

Rigby Focus Forward

Published in 2007 by Nelson Australia Pty Ltd ACN: 058 280 149
A Cengage Learning company

1 2 3 4 5 6 7 8 374 14 13 12 11 10 09 08 07
Printed and bound in China

The Story of Alexander Fleming
ISBN-13 978-1-4190-3831-0
ISBN-10 1-4190-3831-1

Acknowledgments
The author and publisher would like to acknowledge permission to reproduce material from the following sources:
Photographs by Akg-images, pp. 11, 20; Corbis Australia Pty Ltd, pp. 6, 18 left, 22; Emerald City Images/Popperfoto, pp. 7, 12, 23 top; Getty Images, pp. 13, 15-6; Lonely Planet Images/Wayne Walton, p. 23 bottom; Photolibrary, pp. 1, 4-5, 8-10, 14, 17, 18 right; Science & Society Picture Library, p. 21; Wellcome Library, London, p. 19.

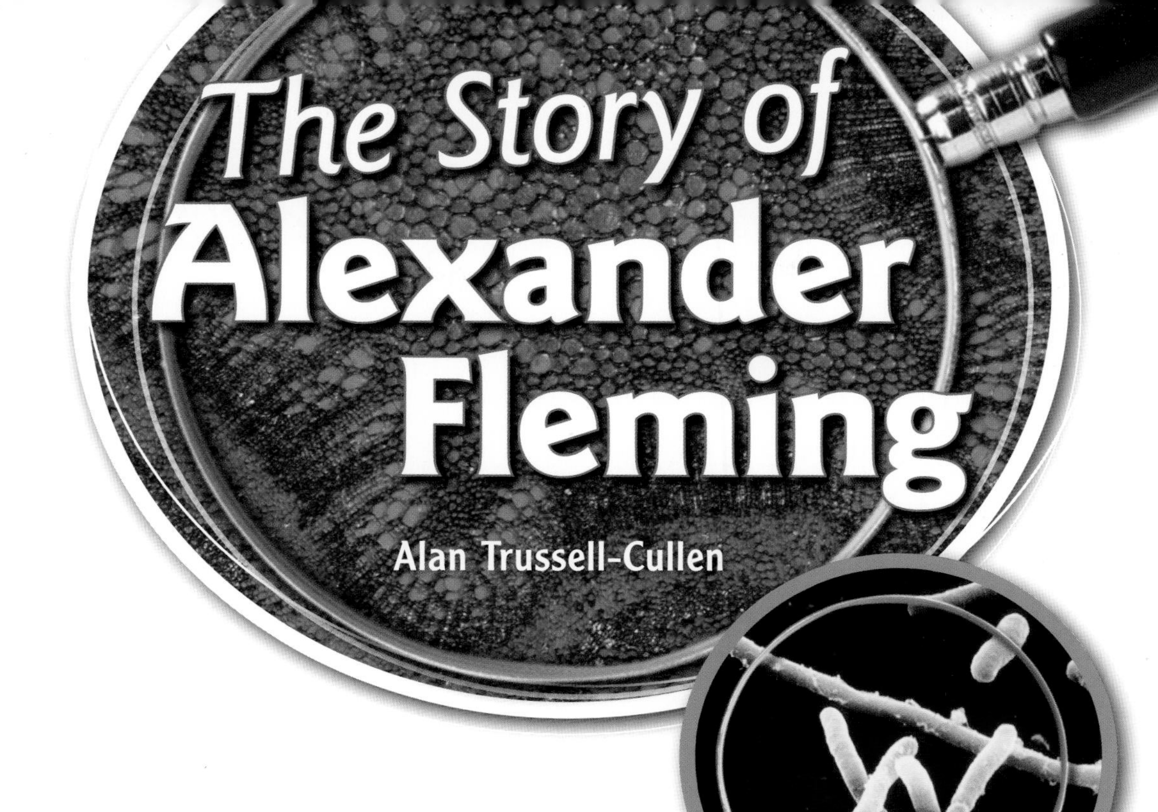

Contents

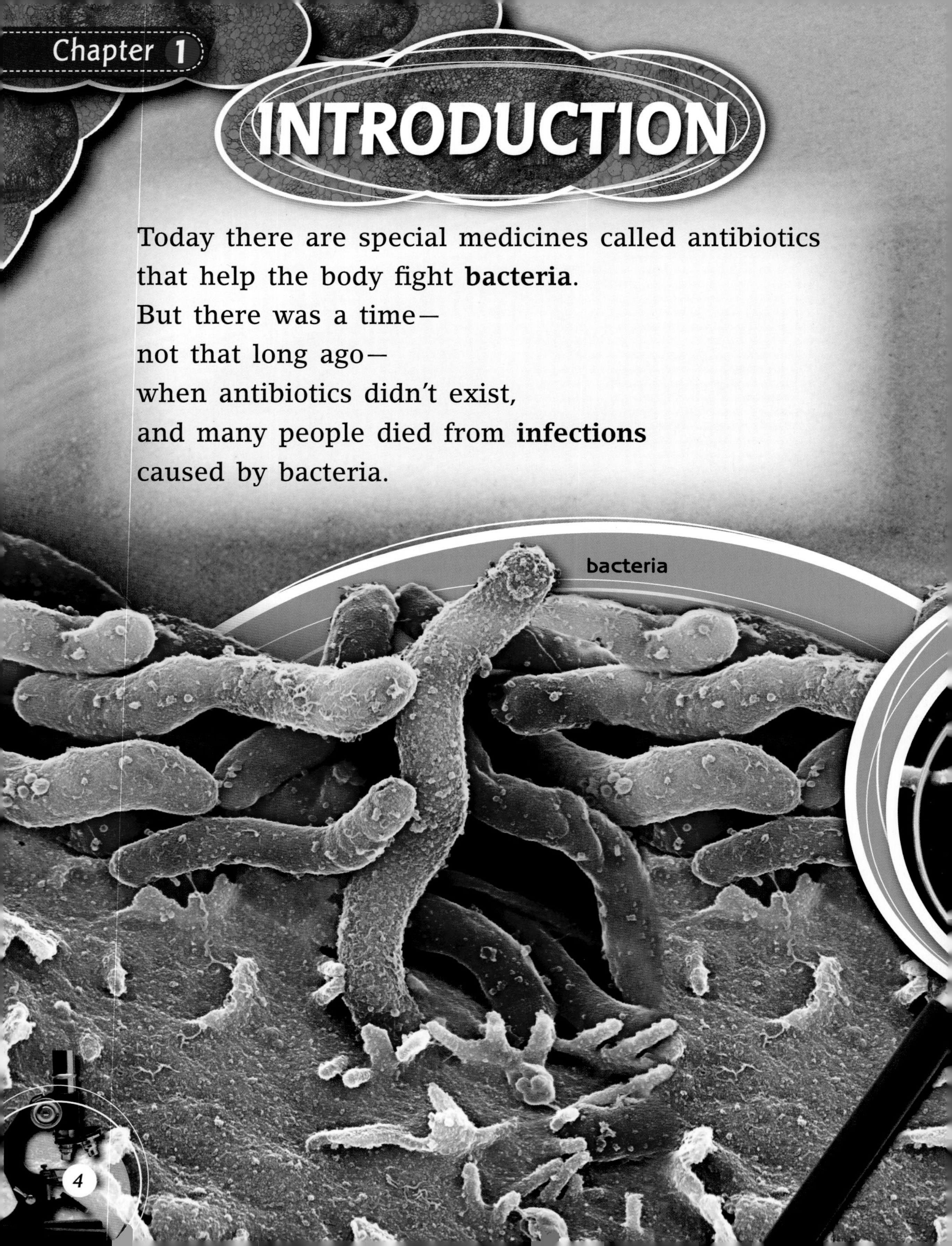

Chapter 1

INTRODUCTION

Today there are special medicines called antibiotics
that help the body fight **bacteria**.
But there was a time—
not that long ago—
when antibiotics didn't exist,
and many people died from **infections**
caused by bacteria.

The world's first antibiotic, called **penicillin**,
was discovered in September 1928
by a doctor, Alexander Fleming.
Fleming's discovery would change medicine forever
and save millions of lives.

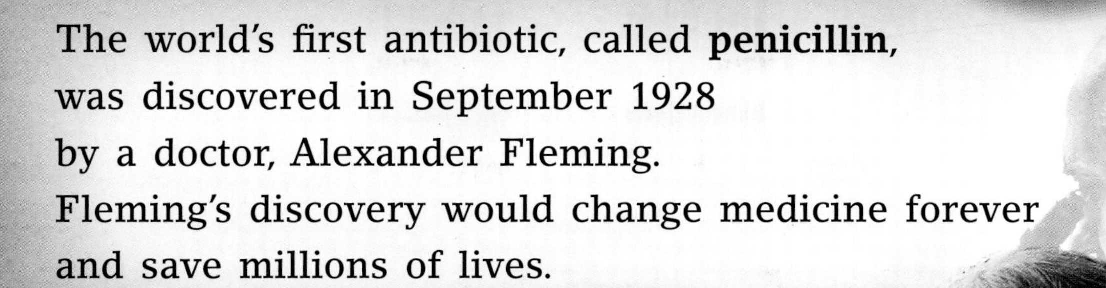

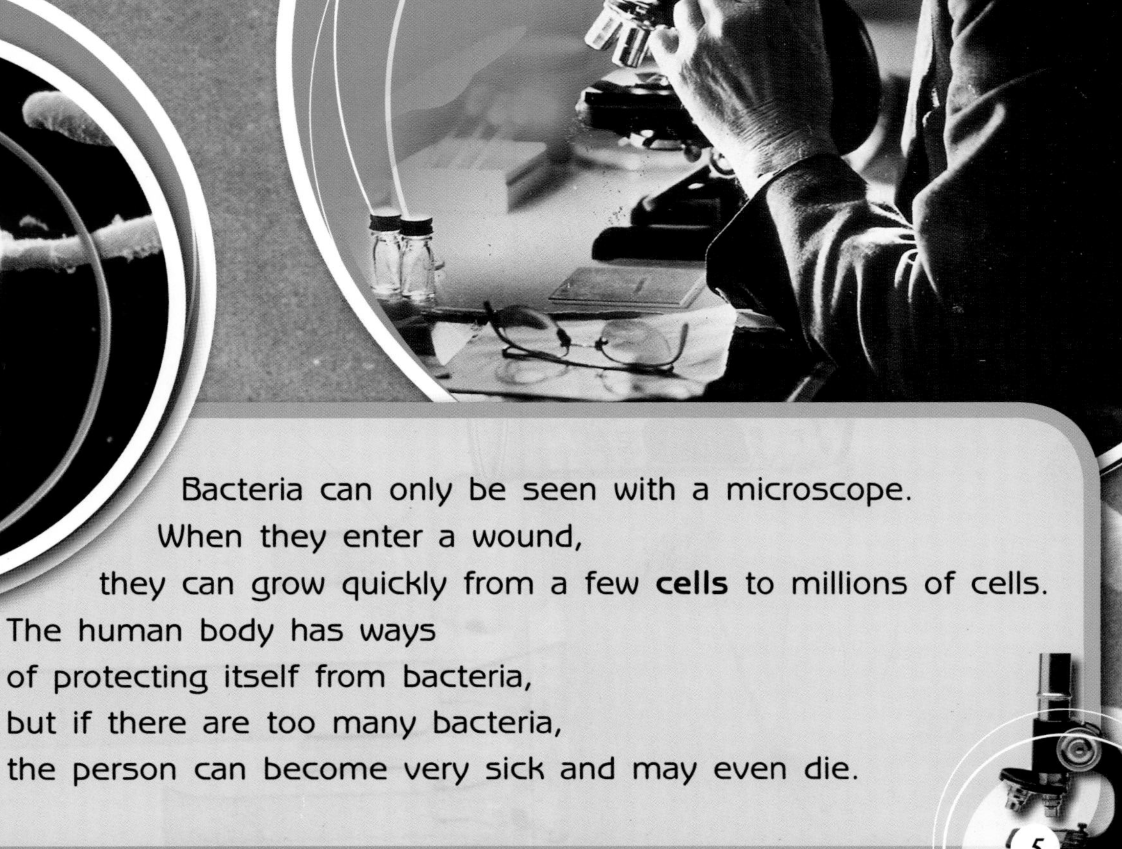

Bacteria can only be seen with a microscope.
When they enter a wound,
they can grow quickly from a few **cells** to millions of cells.
The human body has ways
of protecting itself from bacteria,
but if there are too many bacteria,
the person can become very sick and may even die.

Chapter 2

FLEMING'S EARLY LIFE

Fleming was born on a farm in Scotland in 1881.
He spent many hours playing with his brothers
and sisters and wandering over the countryside.

When Fleming was 14 years old,
he went to live in London with two of his brothers.
At his school in London,
the students laughed at the way he spoke.
But Fleming was bright and loved games.
He quickly made friends.

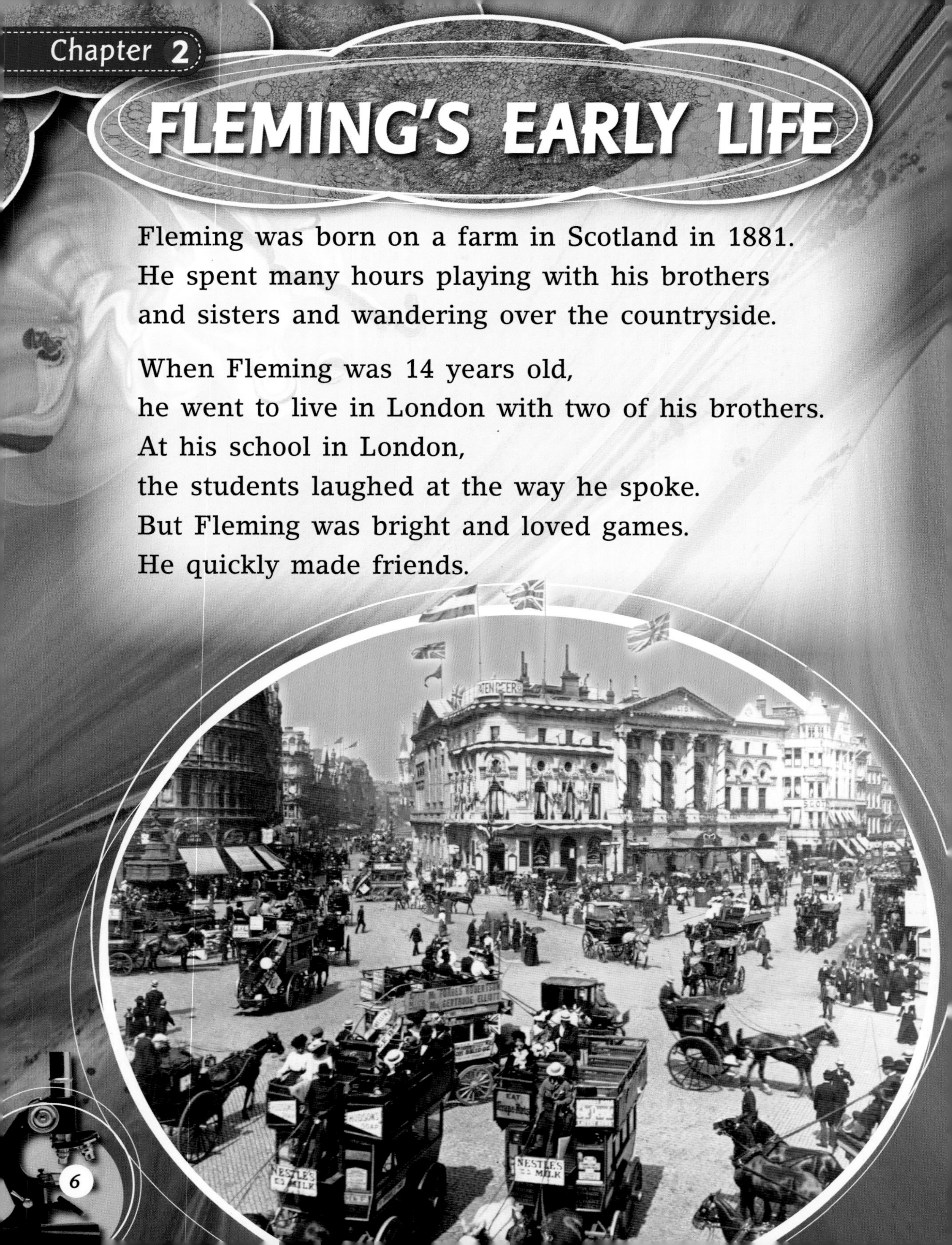

a British Army camp in England

In 1900 Fleming and his brothers joined the army.
While in the army, Fleming found he was good at sports.
He won awards for rifle shooting,
he learned to swim, and he joined a water-polo team.

Love of Sports

Fleming's love of sports played a part in what he wanted to do with his life. In 1901, he decided to become a doctor at St. Mary's Hospital.
He chose to study at St. Mary's because it had a water-polo team!

Fleming's laboratory at St. Mary's Hospital

Fleming in his laboratory

By 1905, Fleming had nearly finished his studies,
and he needed employment.
He wanted to stay at St. Mary's because it had
a rifle-shooting team,
and Fleming was the best on the team!
St. Mary's didn't want to lose him to another hospital,
so they gave him a job in the inoculation department.

Working in the Inoculation Department

Inoculation was new in Fleming's day. Doctors were excited about its development.

Inoculation stops people from getting a disease. Doctors inject people with a weaker form of the bacteria that causes the disease.

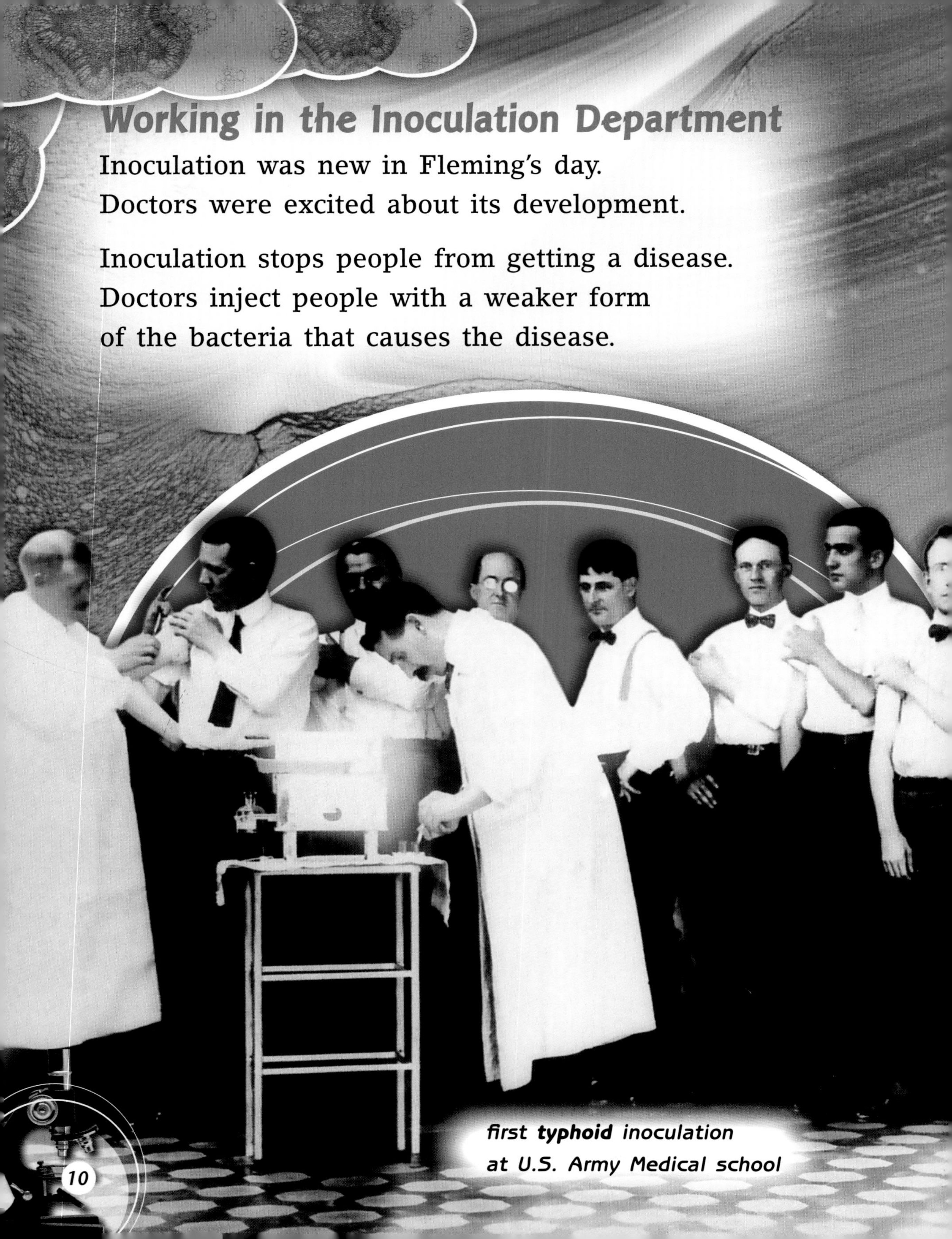

*first **typhoid** inoculation at U.S. Army Medical school*

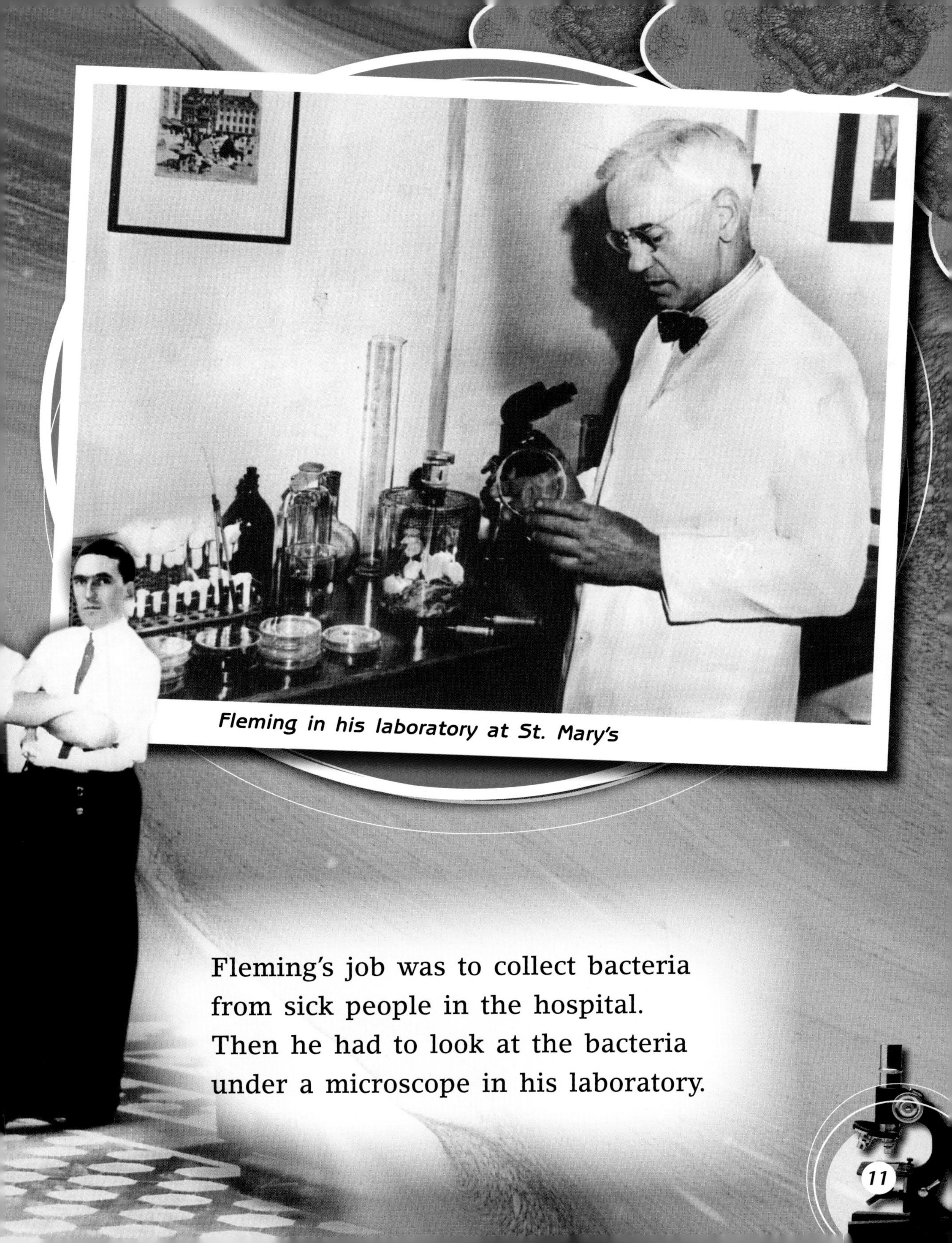

Fleming in his laboratory at St. Mary's

Fleming's job was to collect bacteria from sick people in the hospital. Then he had to look at the bacteria under a microscope in his laboratory.

Chapter 3

WORLD WAR I

World War I began in 1914.
During the war, Fleming went to work in a hospital in France.
There he saw that many soldiers died
not from their wounds,
but from infections in their wounds.

injured soldiers

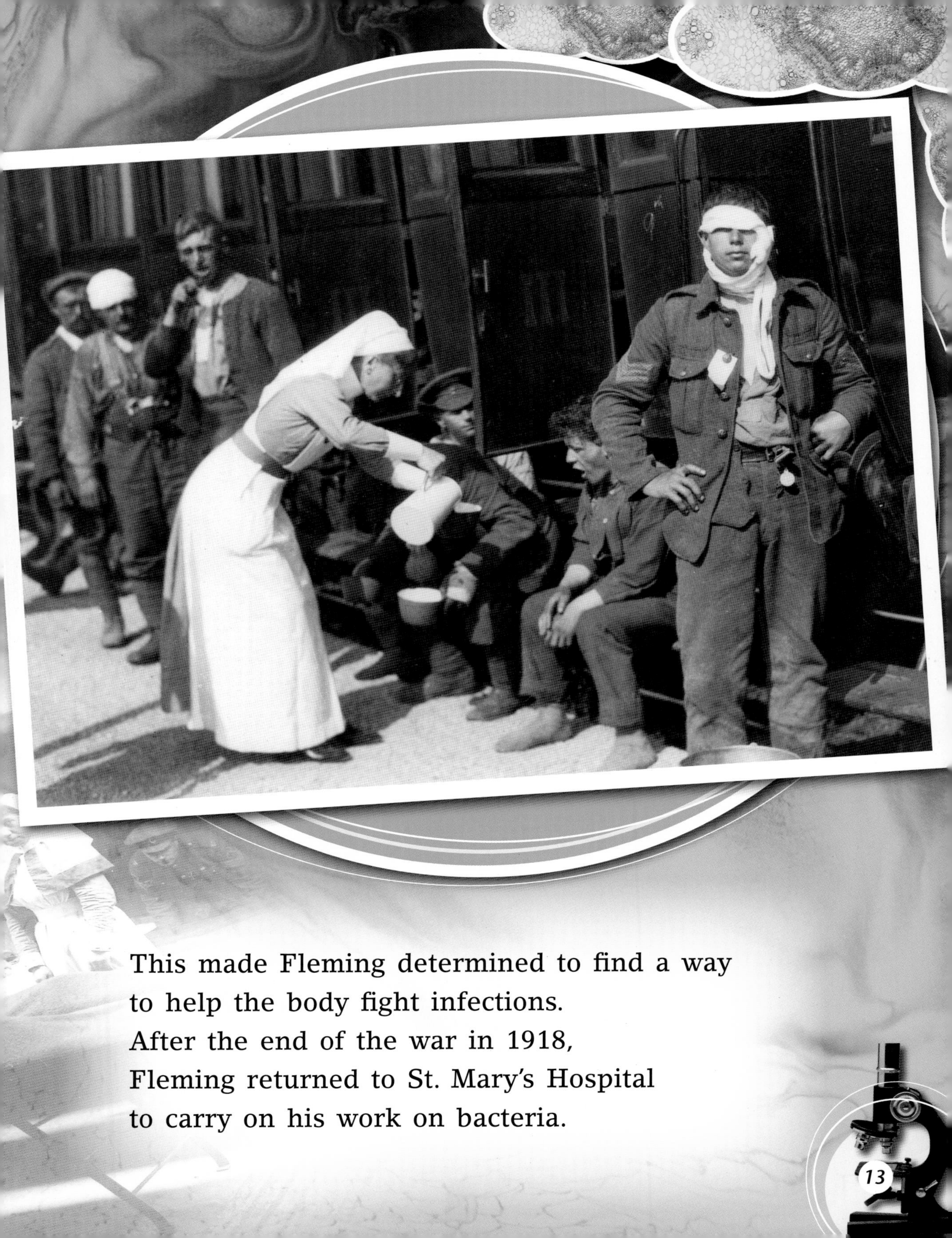

This made Fleming determined to find a way to help the body fight infections. After the end of the war in 1918, Fleming returned to St. Mary's Hospital to carry on his work on bacteria.

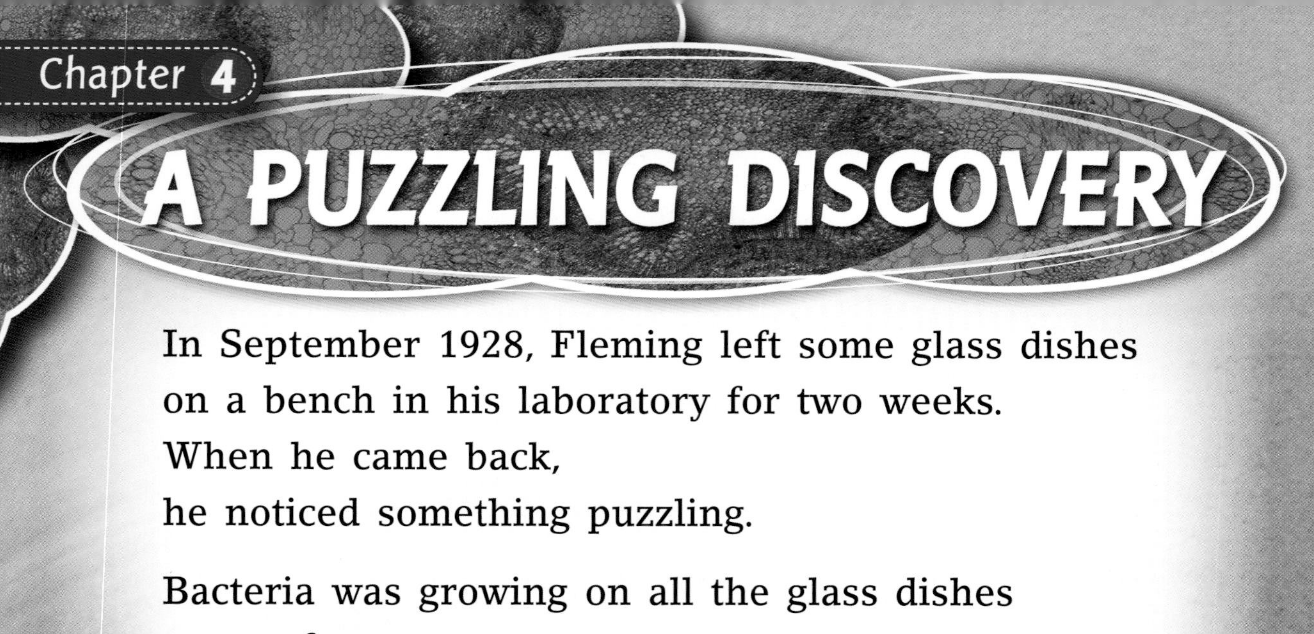

Chapter 4

A PUZZLING DISCOVERY

In September 1928, Fleming left some glass dishes
on a bench in his laboratory for two weeks.
When he came back,
he noticed something puzzling.

Bacteria was growing on all the glass dishes
except for one.
Mold had started to grow on this dish—
the kind found on old bread.

moldy bread

mold growing on Fleming's glass dish

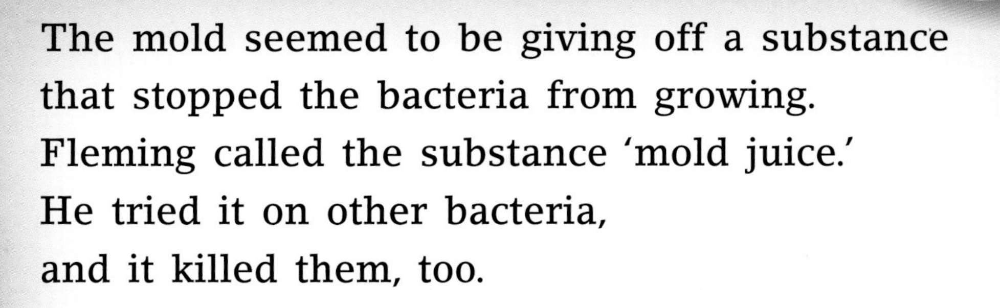

The mold seemed to be giving off a substance
that stopped the bacteria from growing.
Fleming called the substance 'mold juice.'
He tried it on other bacteria,
and it killed them, too.

Fleming was very excited.
He decided to name the substance **penicillin**
because the mold was called *penicillium notatum*.

Fleming tried to get his boss at St. Mary's interested in penicillin.
Unfortunately, Fleming's boss thought that Fleming's work was pointless.
Like many doctors at that time, Fleming's boss thought finding a way to kill bacteria was hopeless.

Fleming explains to Turkish doctors how to make penicillin from mold.

Fleming did a few more experiments with penicillin, and he also wrote about it so other scientists could learn about it.
But because no one seemed interested in his discovery, he forgot about penicillin and started to work on other things.

Chapter 5

THE WORK OF CHAIN AND FLOREY

In 1939, Ernest Chain, a scientist, discovered Fleming's notes. Chain and his boss, Howard Florey, were looking for medicines that could kill bacteria. They decided to test penicillin.

Ernest Chain

Howard Florey

But Florey's team found it hard to grow
enough penicillin for their tests.
They tried growing it in different kinds of trays,
boxes, and even bottles,
but it grew very slowly.
Then one day, they tried growing it in a hospital bedpan.
It worked, and the mold began to grow.

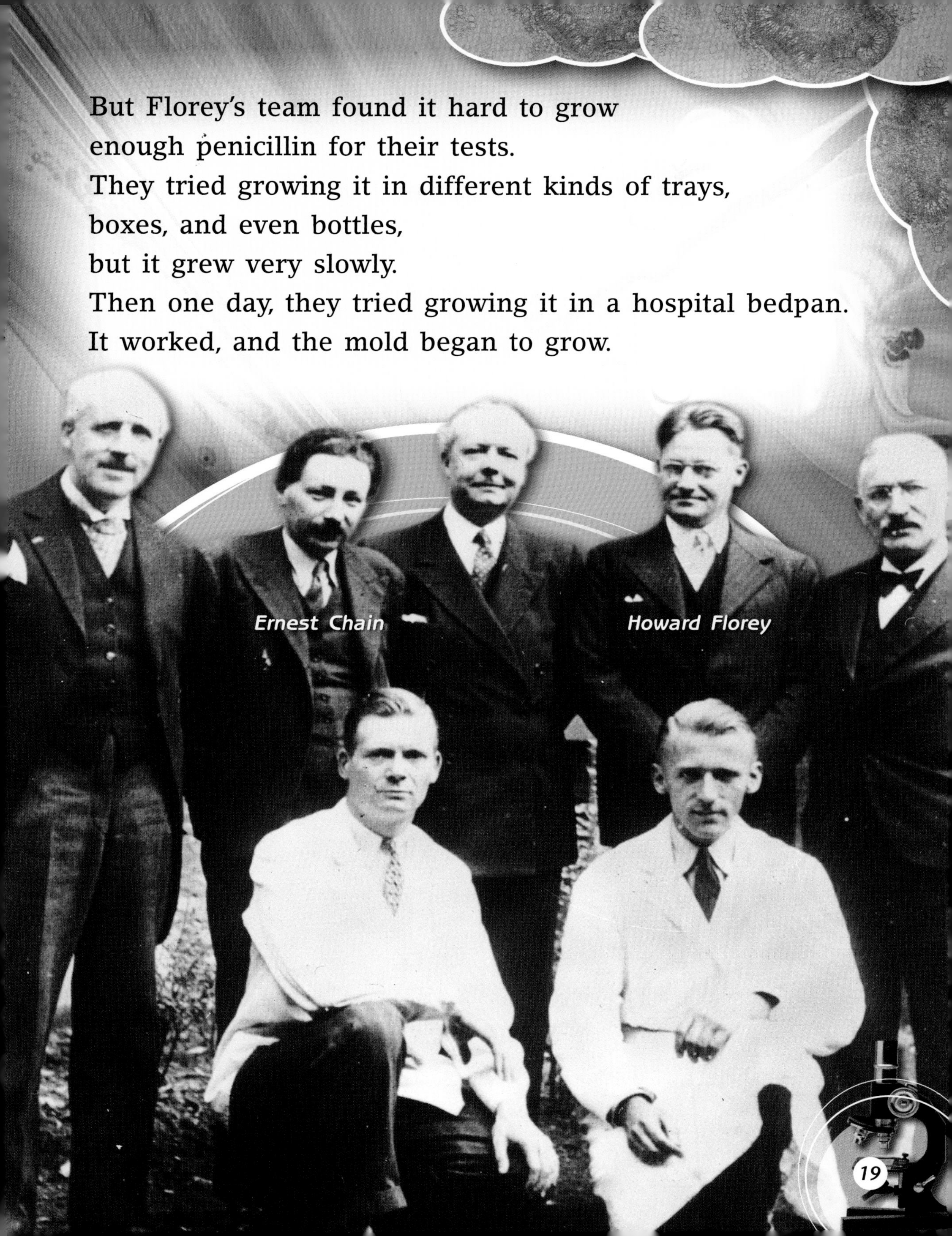

In May 1940, Chain and Florey
decided to experiment with penicillin.
They gave penicillin to some sick mice,
while they didn't give penicillin to some other sick mice.
The mice that were given penicillin survived,
but the ones that didn't get penicillin died.
Florey declared, "It looks like a miracle!"

Ernest Chain

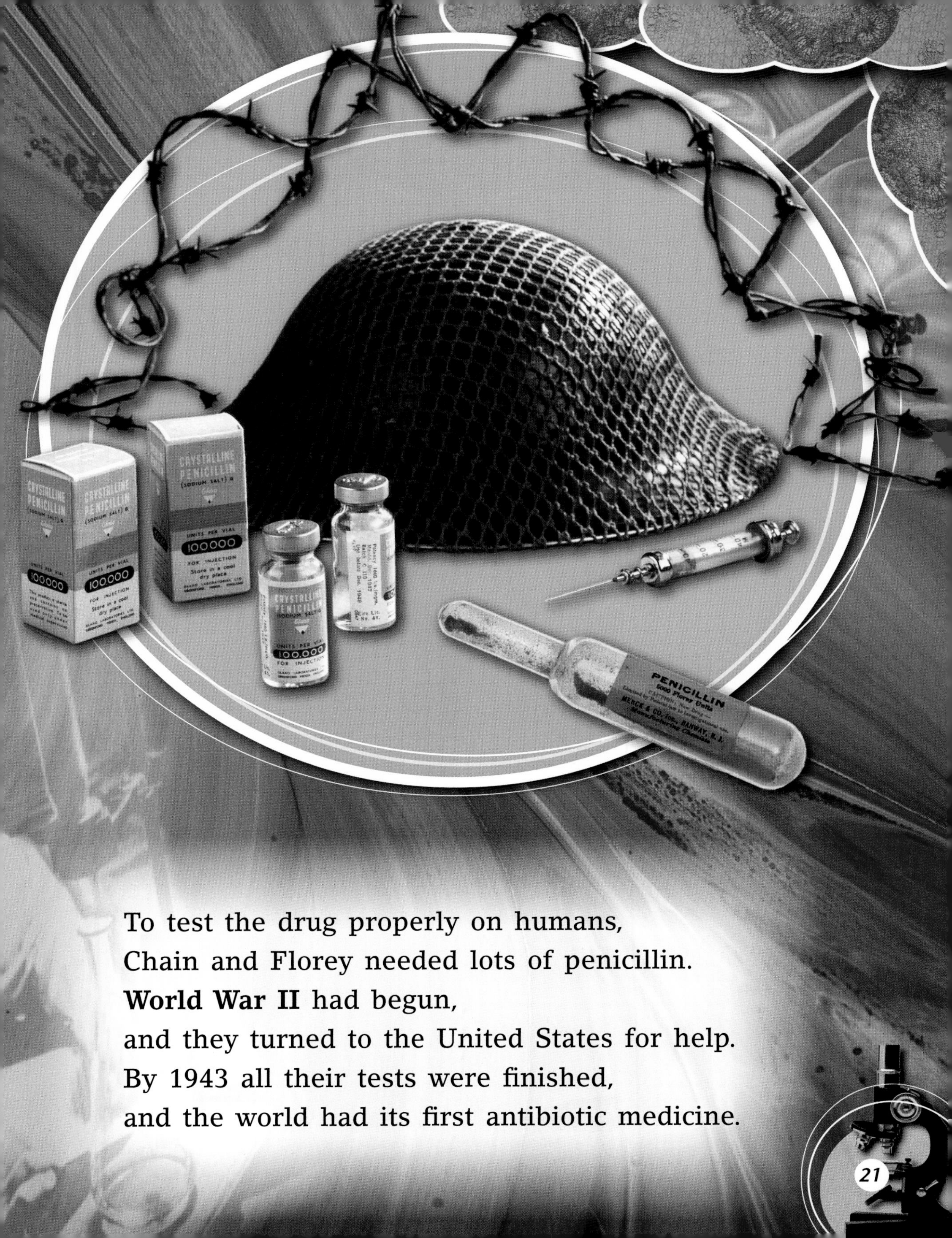

To test the drug properly on humans,
Chain and Florey needed lots of penicillin.
World War II had begun,
and they turned to the United States for help.
By 1943 all their tests were finished,
and the world had its first antibiotic medicine.

Chapter 6

CONCLUSION

Fleming received awards for his work
in discovering penicillin.
He was proud of what he had done,
but he gave endless praise to Chain and Florey
for their work.
In 1945, they all shared the **Nobel Prize**
for their important work.

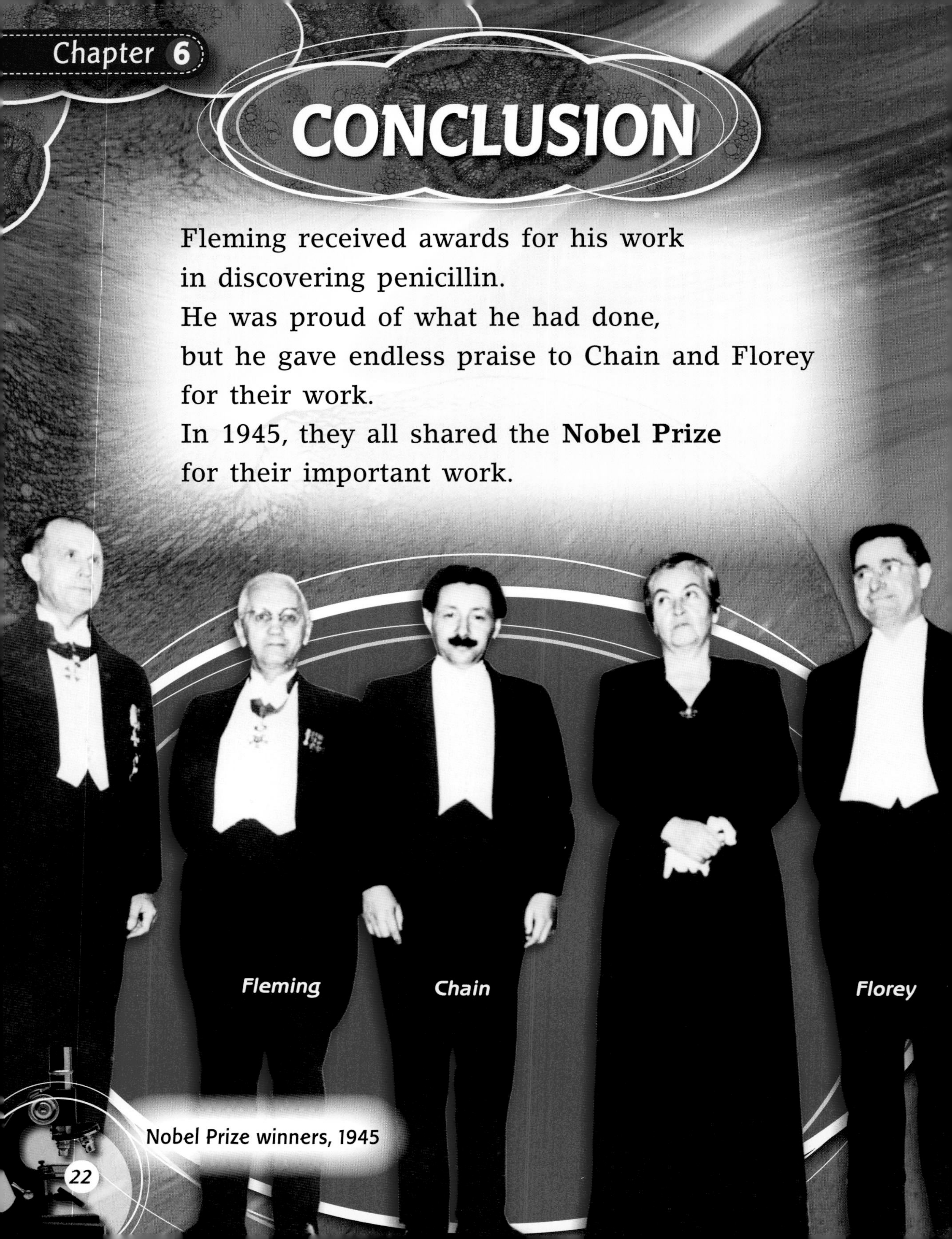

Nobel Prize winners, 1945

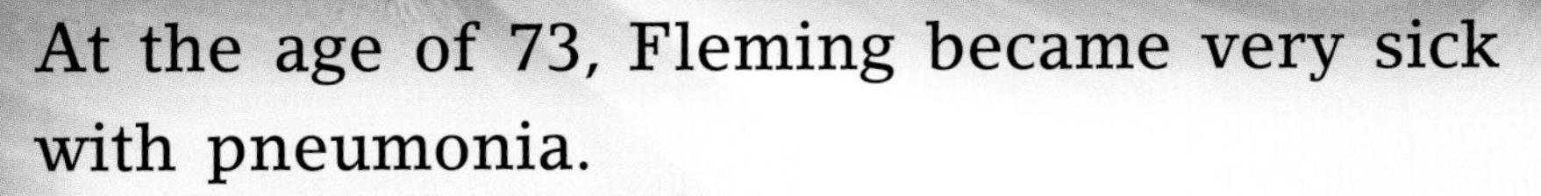

At the age of 73, Fleming became very sick with pneumonia.
Thanks to penicillin, he survived.
Fleming died in 1955 and was buried in St. Paul's Cathedral, alongside other great British heroes.

Glossary

bacteria single cell micro-organisms. Many bacteria cause diseases and infections.

cells the structural and functional units of all living things. Cells are called the "building blocks of life."

infections bacteria that has spread and multiplied causing sickness or death

Nobel Prize an international prize awarded annually for outstanding work in chemistry, physics, literature, peace, physiology, or medicine

penicillin an antibiotic produced naturally by certain molds and used in the treatment of bacterial infections

typhoid a bacterial infection causing fever, red spots on the chest and abdomen, and severe intestinal pain. If left untreated, typhoid can cause death.

World War I a world war fought between 1914 and 1918

World War II a world war fought between 1939 and 1945

Index